LEAVING NO FOOTPRINT
Stories from Asia

At the centre of each of these stories is a family. Husbands and wives, mothers and sons, mothers and daughters – all families have the same problems, the same worries, the same arguments. Nimei in northern China has been married for seventeen years, but a letter from an old flame in her past turns her life upside down. In Singapore, Mr Li is caught between the past and the future, between his old mother and her memories, and his modern young daughter. He wants to be a respectful son, but he does not understand his mother's needs . . . High in the Himalayas, Pritam understands her mother very well, perhaps too well. Her mother does not understand Pritam at all, but only knows that she misses her daughter and wants to be close to her, as all mothers do . . .

BOOKWORMS WORLD STORIES

English has become an international language, and is used on every continent, in many varieties, for all kinds of purposes. *Bookworms World Stories* are the latest addition to the Oxford Bookworms Library. Their aim is to bring the best of the world's stories to the English language learner, and to celebrate the use of English for storytelling all around the world.

Jennifer Bassett
Series Editor

Coming was an empty promise,
you have gone, and left no footprint:
the moonlight slants above the roof,
already the fifth watch sounds.
Dreams of remote partings,
cries which cannot summon,
hurrying to finish the letter,
ink which will not thicken . . .

Li Shangyin (812–56) Late T'ang Dynasty
Translated by A. C. Graham

OXFORD BOOKWORMS LIBRARY
World Stories

Leaving No Footprint

Stories from Asia

Stage 3 (1000 headwords)

Series Editor: Jennifer Bassett
Founder Editor: Tricia Hedge
Activities Editors: Jennifer Bassett and Christine Lindop

NOTES ON THE ILLUSTRATORS

KIM SENG (illustrations on pages 3, 6, 11, 14, 17, 21, 24, 29, 34, 36) was born in Vietnam, and is half Chinese, half Cambodian. He arrived in New Zealand as a refugee at the age of four, and now lives in Wellington, where he studied illustration at Massey University. He is passionate about using illustrations to convey stories and ideas. These are his first illustrations for a book for English language learners.

PRASHANT MIRANDA (illustrations on pages 40, 45, 49, 53, 56) was born in Quilon, India, grew up in Bangalore, and studied animation film design in Ahmedabad. He now lives for six months a year in Canada, and spends the winters in India. He records his life through his watercolour journals, and his work includes watercolour paintings and making watercolour animation films. These are his first illustrations for a book for English language learners.

RETOLD BY CLARE WEST

Leaving No Footprint

Stories from Asia

OXFORD UNIVERSITY PRESS

OXFORD
UNIVERSITY PRESS

Great Clarendon Street, Oxford OX2 6DP

Oxford University Press is a department of the University of Oxford.
It furthers the University's objective of excellence in research, scholarship,
and education by publishing worldwide in

Oxford New York

Auckland Cape Town Dar es Salaam Hong Kong Karachi
Kuala Lumpur Madrid Melbourne Mexico City Nairobi
New Delhi Shanghai Taipei Toronto

With offices in

Argentina Austria Brazil Chile Czech Republic France Greece
Guatemala Hungary Italy Japan Poland Portugal Singapore
South Korea Switzerland Thailand Turkey Ukraine Vietnam

OXFORD and OXFORD ENGLISH are registered trade marks of
Oxford University Press in the UK and in certain other countries

ISBN: 978 0 19 479141 0

A complete recording of this Bookworms edition of
Leaving No Footprint: Stories from Asia is available in an audio CD pack ISBN 978 0 19 479353 7

Printed in China

ACKNOWLEDGEMENTS
*The publishers are grateful to the following
for permission to adapt and simplify copyright texts:*
The author for *Flame* from *The Bridegroom* by Ha Jin first published by
William Heinemann of Random House Group Ltd. in 2000; the author
for *Tanjong Rhu* from *Tanjong Rhu and other stories* by Minfong Ho;
the author for *In the Mountains* from *How I Became a Holy Mother
and other stories* by Ruth Prawer Jhabvala

Word count (main text): 11,546 words

For more information on the Oxford Bookworms Library,
visit www.oup.com/bookworms

CONTENTS

NOTE ON THE LANGUAGE

There are many varieties of English spoken in the world, and the characters in these stories from Asia sometimes use structures, word order, or expressions not found in other varieties of English. This is how the authors of the original stories represented the spoken language that their characters would actually use in real life.

Flame

HA JIN
❧

A story from China, retold by Clare West

When we are young, love burns in us like a fire. The flames are bright, beautiful, painful – all at the same time.

Nimei has been married for seventeen years to Jiang Bing. She did not choose him; her mother chose him for her. Nimei's heart was with another, a flame that has long been quiet and still – but not forgotten . . .

A letter was lying on Nimei's desk. It puzzled her. From the envelope she could see it came from Harbin, but she knew nobody in that city. She opened the envelope, and wondered if she recognized the squarish handwriting. She turned to the end of the letter to see who the sender was. When she saw the name Hsu Peng, her heart began to beat very fast. She had not heard from him for seventeen years.

He wrote: 'I have learned from a friend that you work at the Central Hospital. I am happy that I have found you at last. I shall be at a meeting in your city at the end of September. For old time's sake I hope you will let me visit you and your family.' He said nothing about his wife, but told Nimei that he had three children – two girls and one boy. He added that he was the commissar of an army division, living at the barracks in Harbin. At the bottom of his letter, he gave her the address of his office.

Nimei locked the letter away in a drawer in her desk. It was already early September. If she wished to meet Hsu Peng, she should write him back soon. But she was unsure why he wanted to see her.

The door opened and Wanyan, a young nurse, came in. 'Nimei,' she said, 'the patient in Room 3 wants to see you.'

'What happened?' she asked worriedly.

'I've no idea. He only wants to see the head nurse.'

The patient in Room 3 was a director in the local government offices. He had had a stomach operation two weeks ago, and for another week he had to stay on a liquid diet. Nimei got up and walked to the door, while putting on her white coat.

In Room 3, the patient was sitting in bed, with his head bent over a magazine and a pencil in his hand. 'Director Liao, how are you today?' Nimei asked pleasantly.

'Fine.' He put the magazine on his bedside table.

'Did you have a good rest?' she asked.

'Yes, I slept two hours after lunch.'

'Are you eating well?'

'Yes, but I'm tired of all this liquid food.'

She smiled. 'Watery rice and egg-drop soup don't taste very good.'

'They're not bad, but it's hard to eat them every day. Can I have something else for a change?'

'What would you like?'

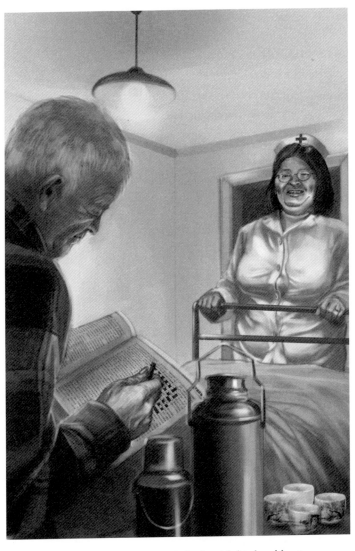

*The patient was sitting in bed, with his head bent
over a magazine and a pencil in his hand.*

'Fish – a soup or a stew.'

Nimei looked at her watch. 'It may be too late for this evening, but I'll go and tell the kitchen manager.'

Director Liao thanked her, although he didn't look happy. Nimei noticed this, but she pretended she hadn't. One of the hospital leaders had informed her that the nurses should take special care of Liao, because he was an important person. She didn't worry too much about that, because there were too many other patients to think about. She went straight downstairs to the kitchen and told the manager to have a fish stew made for the patient the next day. All this time, she couldn't stop thinking about Hsu Peng's letter. She returned to the office, took it out of her desk, and read it again before she left for home.

Walking along Peace Avenue, she was thinking of Hsu Peng. The noise of heavy traffic was all around her, but Nimei's thoughts were far away. She and Hsu Peng had been in love once. That was seventeen years ago, in her home village. After her father died, many people told her mother she could marry Nimei off cheaply. But Nimei's mother refused, saying that her daughter had already given her heart to a man. The villagers believed her. They often saw Jiang Bing visiting. He was a young army officer who worked in the kitchen at the barracks nearby. Through dirty windows, many eyes watched this small man arrive, always with a parcel under his arm. 'That must be some tasty food from the army kitchen!' the villagers whispered to each other.

For two years, bad weather had destroyed most of the

food that was grown in the village, and they were all hungry. A number of people had even died because of poor diet. So they thought Nimei was a lucky girl – she was going to marry an officer who could always find food.

It was true that Nimei had lost her heart to a man, but it was not Jiang Bing. In secret she was meeting Hsu Peng at Snake Mouth Lake every Tuesday afternoon. He was also an army officer, but was much better educated than most of the other army men. So when her mother said she should marry Jiang Bing, Nimei replied, 'But I don't really know him! In fact, I love another man. He's an officer, too.'

'Huh!' answered her mother crossly. 'Love? What's love? You'll learn how to love your man after you marry him. I never even met your father before our wedding.'

Nimei asked her mother to meet Hsu Peng. He's so polite and good-looking – I'm sure she'll like him if she sees him, she thought. But her mother refused, and Jiang Bing continued his visits. He seemed almost like one of the family. Every Saturday Nimei's mother looked forward to seeing what he had brought – sometimes a piece of cooked meat, sometimes dried vegetables or rice. Their neighbours' kitchens were empty and cold, but Nimei and her mother never went hungry. On Sundays, there was always smoke coming from their chimney, and the village children used to stand outside the house, smelling the delicious air.

This made Nimei's mother very happy, and she wanted to give her daughter to Jiang Bing. One evening, she started crying and, through her tears, said again and again, 'Please, Nimei! You must marry this man who can save us!'

*Nimei turned and ran away, tears running down her face
in the autumn wind.*

A daughter must respect her mother's wishes, and finally, Nimei had to agree.

When she told Hsu Peng that she had to obey her mother and marry the other man, he said, with an angry light in his eyes, 'I hate you! I'll get my revenge!'

She turned and ran away, tears running down her face in the autumn wind. Those were his last words to her.

Nimei and Jiang Bing married soon afterwards. They moved into the city when he left the army. But Nimei never forgot Hsu Peng's angry words and his crazy, staring eyes.

At night, awake and lonely, she used to wonder where he was. Was his wife kind-hearted and pretty? Was he still in the army? Had he forgotten her?

Although she thought of him often, she had dreamed of him only twice. Once he appeared in her dream as a farmer; he looked strong and healthy, and owned a five-room house with a red roof. In her other dream he was bald, a teacher in a school for young children. Afterwards she was a little saddened that he looked so old. But who wouldn't change in seventeen years? Her own body was thick and roundish now, the shape of a large fruit. Her face was fatter, and she wore glasses. What hadn't changed was her sighing in the darkness while her husband slept in the other bed in their room. What stayed with her were Hsu Peng's last words, which seemed to echo in her head more loudly every year.

'Want some tea?' Jiang Bing asked Nimei.

'Yes.' She was lying on her bed, with both hands under her neck. She had come home two hours ago.

'Here you are.' He put a cup of tea on the bedside table and walked out, his back a little bent. He was helping their daughter with her studies. This autumn she needed to do well enough to get into nursing school. In the living room, Nimei's mother and Nimei's eleven-year-old son, Songshan, were laughing at a TV programme together. Outside, the night air smelled of vegetables cooking.

Why does Hsu Peng want to see me? Nimei wondered. Didn't he hate me? Maybe he no longer hates me, but surely he must hate my mother and Jiang Bing. It's good that they've never met. Why is he eager to visit me and my family after so many years? Does this mean he still feels something for me? Is the old flame still burning? If he knew what I look like now . . .

She turned from side to side, unable to rest. Then she had a thought. Didn't he say he was a commissar? He must have a very high rank in the army. Is this his revenge – showing me, to my face, how important he is? If he visits us, I'll be so ashamed. Our house is shabby. My husband is just an office worker at the hospital – why couldn't he get a job a few ranks higher? What a useless man he is.

But there's one good thing, Nimei thought. After Hsu Peng's visit, I can tell my mother who this commissar is. The old woman will be sorry that she made me marry Jiang Bing. That will teach her a lesson.

Nimei said nothing to her family, and wrote to Hsu Peng the next day, inviting him to visit her and her family. She even wrote: 'For old time's sake, please come to see me. I miss you.' On the envelope she put a special stamp, a Youth

Day stamp, which showed a young man and a girl dancing.

At lunchtime Nimei went to the bathroom on the third floor of the hospital building. She stared at her face in the mirror, sighed, and cleaned her glasses. You have to do something about yourself, she thought. Remember to dye your hair. Also, you must take some exercise. You look fat and unhealthy.

The young nurse, Wanyan, reported that the patient in Room 3 had complained about the fish stew at lunch.

'Don't worry,' said Nimei, 'I'll talk with him and see what I can do. By the way, Wanyan, may I ask you something?'

'Sure, what is it?'

'Can you help me buy five hundred bricks from your brother?'

'Are you going to build something?'

'No. My yard gets so dirty when it rains. I want to put down a brick floor.'

'No problem. My brother will give you a good price.'

'Wonderful. Thank you.'

Nimei went to Room 3. When he saw her, Director Liao began complaining about the fish stew. 'I don't like saltwater fish, you see,' he explained.

'I'll try my best to find freshwater fish,' said Nimei.

Shaking his head, the patient said crossly, 'I can't believe it's so difficult. This city's on the Songhua River! There must be plenty of freshwater fish!'

'I promise I'll find fish for you, Director Liao,' Nimei told him.

That evening Nimei talked with her husband. 'Go to the riverside tomorrow and buy a big fish,' she said.

'River fish are expensive,' said Jiang Bing.

'Don't worry about the money,' replied his wife. 'The money that you spend on the fish will come back to you in the end. Buy the fish, make a stew and take it to my office at the hospital.'

Jiang Bing did not want to argue with her. He remembered she had once burned some of his money because he said he was going to buy her mother an expensive winter coat. He did not want that to happen again.

The next morning Nimei got up early and went for a run on the school playground nearby. It was the first time she put on the sports shoes her husband had bought her three years ago. Jiang Bing was pleased to see that at last she was beginning to take care of her health. He went to the riverside and bought a large whitefish, which he kept alive in a bowl of water.

He left the office early that afternoon, and the moment he reached home, he started work on the fish. He killed and cleaned it. Then slowly and carefully he made a very tasty stew, the best he knew how to make. While it was cooking, he sat outside in the yard, lit a cigarette and gave a toothy smile to Nimei's mother. She was watching him, wide-eyed.

'It's not a holiday today, so why cook the fish in this special way?' asked the old woman.

'My job, Mother. I'm helping Nimei.'

'She's forgotten who she is. She thinks she's a queen, giving orders all the time.'

*It was the first time Nimei put on the sports shoes
her husband had bought her three years ago.*

At five-thirty Jiang Bing arrived at Nimei's office with a large dinner pot. Together they went to Room 3. When he saw the fish stew, the patient's eyes brightened. After trying two spoonfuls, he said, 'What a beautiful job! Who made this?'

'My husband did,' said Nimei. 'He used to work in the kitchen at the barracks when he was in the army, so he knows how to cook fish.'

'Thank you, Young Jiang,' said the patient, eating noisily. He put out his right hand and Jiang Bing shook it.

Every morning from then on, Jiang Bing got up early and went to the riverside to buy fish. Each day he cooked the fish in a different way. But soon Jiang Bing had spent all his pay and Nimei's as well. 'Why don't you go to the bank and take out some of the money we've saved?' Nimei said to him. He agreed, and day after day he continued to cook wonderful fish soups and stews for Liao.

While this was happening, Nimei was taking exercise for half an hour every morning and again later in the day. In ten days' time, she looked much healthier, although she wasn't any thinner. Why didn't you do this years ago? she asked herself. A healthy body must make the heart feel younger.

A few times Director Liao wanted to pay Nimei for the fish, but she refused to accept any money from him. She told him, 'It's my job to take care of my patients.'

Little by little, the director and Jiang Bing got to know each other. Every day after Liao finished dinner, Jiang used to stay by the patient's bedside for an hour or two, and the two men talked. When the nurses asked Nimei why her husband came at dinnertime every day, she said that Liao and Jiang Bing knew each other from before. Of course nobody believed her, but the nurses were just happy that at last the patient was being pleasant and polite to everybody around him. Nimei pretended that Director Liao paid for the fish he ate.

The bricks arrived. Nimei paid for them and gave the driver two packets of Great Production cigarettes.

For a whole weekend Nimei and Jiang Bing worked on their yard. They carefully flattened the ground and then laid the bricks. It was unusually warm weather for autumn, and they were both very hot and tired when they finished. Nimei's mother had made a large pot of soup for them. She added white sugar to the soup and put it into bowls, which were placed on a long table in the yard to get cool.

The work was done and Nimei was pleased, although her back ached. But her mother said, 'Throwing money away! We've never used good bricks like these, even for a house.'

Nimei was too tired to reply. Jiang Bing just drank his soup, his thin shoulders more bent than before. His dirty grey hair lay flat on his head. The back of his shirt was wet and looked like an old map.

Nimei's mother kept saying, 'We'll need a lot of money for winter vegetables, and we ought to save for the spring.'

Be quiet, you awful old woman! thought Nimei.

The next day she bought two large pots of wild roses and had them placed at the entrance to the yard. She told her daughter to water the flowers every morning.

*The next day she bought two large pots of wild roses and
had them placed at the entrance to the yard.*

〰

Director Liao was going to leave the hospital in two days' time. On Tuesday afternoon he had the head nurse called in. 'Nimei, I can't thank you enough,' he said.

'It's my job. Please don't thank me.'

'I've told the hospital what a good nurse you are. You've been kinder to me than my own family! Is there anything I can do for you? I'm really very grateful.'

'No, I don't need anything,' she said. 'Jiang Bing and I are very happy that you've got better so quickly.'

'Ah yes, how about Young Jiang? Can I do something for him?'

She pretended to think for a minute. 'Well, maybe. He's worked in the same office for almost ten years. He may want a change. But don't tell him I said this or he'll be angry with me.'

'I won't say a word. Do you think he wants to leave the hospital?'

'No, he likes it here. Just moving him to another office would be enough. Actually, there are two offices where they don't have a director at the moment.'

'Good. I'm going to write to the hospital leaders. They'll do what I say. Tell Young Jiang I'll miss his fish.'

They both laughed.

Everything's going well, thought Nimei. I've heard from Hsu Peng, who says he'll be happy to come for tea. My daughter has just got a place at a nursing school. And when Jiang Bing becomes a director, he'll be closer in rank to Hsu Peng. Now I won't feel too ashamed to meet him!

🔥

On the evening of September 29, an army car stopped at the entrance to the Jiangs' yard. At the sound of the engine, Nimei checked that her newly-dyed hair was tidy, and went out to welcome the visitor. To her surprise, two soldiers walked into the yard. One was carrying a parcel and the other was holding a large green oil container. 'Is this Head Nurse Nimei's home?' one of them asked.

'Yes,' she said eagerly, her left hand touching the buttons on her new, flowered dress. Her husband came out of the house and joined her.

The taller soldier said, 'Our commissar cannot come this evening. He's very sorry. He has to go with another officer to a party.'

'Oh.' Nimei was too confused to say another word.

The man continued, 'Commissar Hsu ordered us to bring you the fish and the cooking oil for National Day.' They put the parcel and the container on a table in the yard.

'Is he coming to see us?' she asked.

'No. We're leaving for Harbin on the earliest train tomorrow morning.'

'Who's this commissar?' Jiang Bing asked his wife.

'He used to be a patient of mine – I told you,' she managed to reply. She turned to the soldiers. 'Tell your commissar we thank him.'

'How much?' Jiang Bing asked them, still puzzled.

'Our commissar said we mustn't take any money.'

The young men turned and went out. The car engine started up and they drove away.

When the parcel was opened, four very large fish appeared. Nimei's mother was very pleased. Jiang Bing said excitedly, 'They've just come from the river! Too bad that Director Liao has left the hospital. These are the best fish – he'd love them.' He asked his wife, 'Why haven't I ever met this commissar?'

'He's with an army division somewhere in Harbin. The fish and the oil probably didn't cost him anything.' She wanted to cry.

'Of course not. If you have rank, you can always get the best things free.' He waved a fly away with his hand. 'Songshan, get me the largest bowl, quick.'

The boy turned, a half-eaten fruit in his hand, and ran to fetch the bowl.

Nimei couldn't hold back her tears any more. She hurried into the house and threw herself on her bed. She began to cry miserably, wondering if Hsu Peng had ever meant to visit her at all.

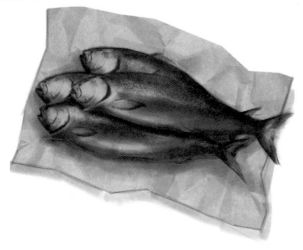

Tanjong Rhu

MINFONG HO

A story from Singapore, retold by Clare West

At Tanjong Rhu in Singapore harbour today, tall office buildings reach to the sky. Eighty years ago there were only small shipyards here, where fishing boats were built, and children looked for crabs along the beach.

Mr Li is a rich, successful, modern business- man, with modern ways and modern ideas. But he is closer to his old mother than he realizes. They see the world in very different ways – or do they?

The day after his mother was buried, Mr T. W. Li stood for a long time looking out of his office window high above Shenton Way. Below him, sunlight fell on the oily water of Singapore harbour. He could hear the noise of heavy traffic in the distance. Only just a quarter past five, and his office was silent; the phones were quiet, the lights were off. It was time to go home.

But Mr Li was not yet ready to go. He was usually a very busy man, but this afternoon he felt he wanted to just look out of his office window a little longer. He was tired, and his tie was loose. Like many people of his age in Singapore, he looked only as old as he chose to. He kept his hair carefully dyed black, except for a little grey. He hoped this made him look like a man who had inherited his money, not earned it.

But this afternoon Mr Li looked older than he liked. Something worried him. It wasn't just that he was saddened by his mother's burial. He had made sure that everything was done in the right way. Even in death, lying in her coffin, his mother looked just as she always did, calm and kind.

What was it, then? Why did he feel that he had left something undone?

He sighed, and looked out of the window again, at the ships waiting in the harbour. There were 68 of them yesterday, thought Mr Li, and 84 the day before. Then he realized that he couldn't remember the number for today. Quickly, he picked up the pair of binoculars near the window and looked through them at the harbour. One by one he counted the ships there: 78 – that was the number for today. He repeated it to himself. Numbers were strong, numbers he could hold on to. 78 ships, 18th floor, 63 years old, these numbers fixed him in place and time.

He looked at the binoculars in his hand. Hadn't he bought them for his mother? Of course, he thought. I bought them for her cataracts, for her to see better, because she didn't want an operation.

He was boyishly eager to show her the binoculars, the evening he returned home from work with them. The driver had only just stopped the Mercedes Benz, when Mr Li jumped out. Pushing past the servant at the door, he hurried towards the back of the house, walking past room after room looking for his mother. He was proud of the house, but he always had the feeling that there were too many empty rooms in it, and most of them too big.

In one of the rooms he saw his wife Helen, having tea with a handful of her friends. He disliked these teas of hers, with the women's soft voices, the smell of perfume, the cakes made with expensive foreign fruit.

'Edward,' she said, crossing her legs, 'come and join us?'

He refused, and was just turning away, when she noticed the binoculars he was holding, and asked what they were.

'Oh, these,' he said. 'I bought them today. For the children.' He could not think of anything better to say.

'Really, Edward,' his wife said, amused. She turned to her friends and smiled. 'Our son's almost finished at Cambridge University, and Ying's about to leave for New York next month, but he still buys toys for them!' Polite laughter from her women friends followed him as he left the room.

He found his mother beside the swimming pool in the garden, where she was feeding her chickens. She was small and thin, with grey hair and a bent back.

'Ah-Ma,' he called.

She lifted her eyes and stared blankly at him. Cloudy with the milky thickness of many years, her eyes stared at everything the same way, calm and blank like windows.

'Ah-Ma, I bought – today – one thing, for you.'

As always, when he went from speaking English all day back to Cantonese, he found it difficult to say what he wanted.

*Mr Li found his mother beside the swimming pool
in the garden, where she was feeding her chickens.*

She smiled at him. 'Ah-Wah,' she said, 'things you can buy, I do not need.' Her voice was low.

'But you don't even know what it is.'

'I know I have everything I need.'

'Everything, Mother? What about your eyes? Wouldn't you like to see clearly?'

'Who says I cannot see now?' she asked crossly. 'Is it that young doctor? Just because I wouldn't tell him what shapes were on that wall picture of his.'

'You want to see better, don't you?' he said quickly.

'I am not, Ah-Wah, having my eyes cut open,' she said.

'I'm not talking about the operation, Ah-Ma . . .'

'Cutting into my eyes with a knife!'

'This has nothing to do with the operation,' he said, and pushed the binoculars into her free hand. 'They're special glasses, see-far glasses to help you see things far away.'

'See-far glasses? What do I want to look at faraway things for?' She went on feeding the chickens, making soft little noises to them.

He looked at her, this little old woman – mother of nine, grandmother of thirty-four, and great-grandmother of seventeen. And she, fixed at their centre, like a tree from which countless fruits had grown. Now, in the back yard of her eldest son's house, she spent her evenings feeding chickens. What, after all, did she need these binoculars for? He turned back towards the house.

'Wait,' she called after him. 'These see-far glasses of yours, can they see Tanjong Rhu?'

He stopped. 'Tanjong Rhu? I suppose they can.'

'If they can see as far away as Tanjong Rhu,' she said, 'I will try them.'

He walked back to her, the eagerness growing in him again. 'From my office window, Ah-Ma,' he said, 'you can see Tanjong Rhu very clearly. I'll take you up there – you've never even been to my office – and we'll look through the see-far glasses at Tanjong Rhu. Would you like that?'

'I would,' she said. 'I have not seen your father's shipyard for a long time.'

'Father's shipyard?'

'The one at Tanjong Rhu. Don't you remember?'

'But Mother, that was pulled down thirty years ago!'

'You said those see-far glasses could see far away, Ah-Wah,' she said.

'Oh Mother,' he sighed. 'You don't understand.'

It was beginning to get dark. 'It's all right. I don't need those glasses of yours,' she said. 'I can see Tanjong Rhu just fine. Behind my eyes, that's how I can still see it.'

'Yes, Ah-Ma,' he said, moving towards the house.

'You remember?' she asked. 'You used to climb inside the empty fishing boats that your father was building. You used to play there with Ah-May and Ah-Lian.'

'Let's go in, Mother.'

'And that little wooden hut that we lived in, remember?'

'I'm going in,' he said. Once she started talking about the old days, who knew how long she would keep going!

'No, Ah-Wah, wait for me,' she said softly. 'I've finished.'

He offered her his arm and together they walked to the house. 'Maybe I *will* go take a look,' she said. 'Even if I

Mr Li went back to the altar room and found his daughter and his mother arguing over some joss sticks.

cannot see where your father worked, I can see where you work.' The servant opened the door for them. 'Tomorrow morning, then,' his mother said. 'Perhaps you'll show me Tanjong Rhu after all?' And with that, she stepped inside.

The next morning, on his way downstairs to breakfast, he saw her in the dark little room where the family altar was. 'Ah-Ma,' he called, 'remember – you are coming with me today!'

There was no reply. She was cleaning the altar and putting new flowers on it. He tried to talk to her again, but this time she cut him short.

'If we have to do something,' she said, in the loud, serious voice she always used in the altar room, 'we must do it right. If I am to visit your place of work, I must tell your father about it.' Carefully she unlocked the top drawer of her special desk, where she kept everything she needed for the altar: small wine cups, gold sheets, candles and joss sticks. When the grandchildren were younger, they used to help. Ying especially loved helping her grandmother fill the wine cups or burn the gold paper in front of the altar.

'Baba,' he heard Ying call now, 'your food's getting cold.'

He went to have his breakfast. After he had finished his second cup of coffee and read right through the *Asian Wall Street Journal*, he sent Ying to hurry her grandmother up.

Minutes later, he looked at his watch. It was now 8.34 – time to leave. He went back to the altar room and found his daughter and his mother arguing over some joss sticks.

'Let me do it, Popo,' Ying was saying. 'You're so slow!'

'You don't know how to do it,' replied her grandmother.

'Sure I do. It's easy.'

'Yes? How many times do you bow?'

'What does it matter? Come on, Popo, just let me do it.' She noticed her father in the doorway and gave him a secret smile. Softly, in English, she said to him, 'Sorry, this is going to take a long time!' Then, in Cantonese, she said to her grandmother, 'Grandfather would probably like to hear from me for a change. You're the only one who talks to him.'

'Do you even know how to speak to your grandfather in the right way? And afterwards, what candles do you light, what wine do you offer? Do you know?'

Ying sighed deeply. 'It doesn't matter. My father's waiting for you. You'll make him late for work.'

'Tell your father,' the old lady said, 'that *his* father is waiting for me.'

Ying whispered to her father in English, 'She just won't hurry, Baba. Always has to do just what she wants!'

Mr Li frowned. She shouldn't speak like that about her grandmother, he thought. Children these days have no respect for their elders. Aloud, he said in Cantonese, 'Your grandmother is old. She has eaten more salt than you have eaten rice.'

He looked up at the photograph of his father on the altar, lit by a pair of electric candles. For years his mother had refused to use anything except real candles. But when she had almost set fire to the whole altar, she had finally agreed to change to these electric things.

He watched as the old woman bowed in front of the altar, holding the joss sticks in her hands. 'Hear me, respected father of my son,' she called. 'Ah-Wah is taking me to see his place of work today, a beautiful room with windows at the edge of the sky.'

Ying shook her head and tried to leave, but her father held her arm. 'You stay and listen to this,' he whispered.

'He is rich now,' the old woman said, 'and his office is high up, on top of the sea. He says he can see Tanjong Rhu from there, so I will go up and look for it too. Perhaps, father of Ah-Wah, I will see you there.'

The man in the photograph looked down at him, his face smooth and ageless. When he died, he was ten years younger than Li was now. Suddenly Mr Li wanted to speak to his father again, the way he used to, talking away in quick Cantonese, his words only just keeping up with his steps as he ran alongside his father. But now, the words would not come, and his father was gone. So he stayed silent, waiting as his mother slowly put everything away in her desk and locked up the drawer.

She had not been able to see any of the ships, of course, not even with the binoculars. Standing at his office window, she did her best to look through them.

'It's lovely,' she had said, but he could see the binoculars were pointing at clouds in the blue sky. There was a smell of joss sticks on her hair.

'Not there, Ah-Ma,' he said. 'Look down.'

'Oh yes, I think I see – well, what am I supposed to see?'

'The ships, Mother. The big ships out in the harbour. Right in front of you.' How could she not see them, he thought, when I count them every morning without the stupid glasses?

'Many of them, Ah-Wah,' she said. 'Everywhere they are.' But she had moved her head away from the binoculars and was staring blankly in front of her.

Almost roughly, he pushed her head back towards the lenses of the binoculars. 'Look through them,' he said. 'Can't you see? The whole view of the harbour? Don't look at me, look out there! What do you see?'

She was silent. 'Nothing,' she finally said.

He took hold of her thin shoulders and turned her round to look at the far right of the harbour. 'That's Tanjong Rhu over there, Mother. Can you see it? Those glasses are strong, Ah-Ma. You must be able to see *something*?'

She held the binoculars to her eyes for a long time. Then she smiled. 'Oh yes,' she said happily, 'I see, I see it now.'

'What, Ah-Ma?'

'A thin little boy,' she said, her voice shaking, 'in a dirty shirt, with no shoes. Walking alone on the beach. Throwing stones into the sea. Counting the fishing boats near the shipyard.' She laughed, and her laugh was strong. 'I see you, Ah-Wah, I see you so clearly.'

'Mother,' he said, and tried to pull the binoculars away from her. But she held on to them.

'I see our hut by the sea, among the half-built fishing boats. And I see myself too, walking along the beach with you. There's that old basket on my arm, and it's half-filled with crabs that you and I have caught. How you run, Ah-Wah, and dig for the crabs!'

'And I see myself too, walking along the beach with you.
How you run, Ah-Wah, and dig for the crabs!'

'That's enough, Mother,' he said. 'Give those glasses back to me now.'

This time she let him take the binoculars. And when she lifted her eyes to his, they were as blank as office windows, and the smile had disappeared from her old face.

He looked at the binoculars now, lying next to the window. Ah-Ma, he thought, what could you see that morning? Was it really our Tanjong Rhu?

Suddenly he wanted, more than anything in the world, to go back to that time when he was a little boy growing up in Tanjong Rhu. He wanted to see the fishing boats sailing into Tanjong Rhu in the early evening, the wind catching their sails. Closer at home, there was always the smell of salt and fish and rice cooking over wood fires. And yes, he remembered the feel of the sand on the beach between his toes, and the coldness of seaweed around his ankles.

Had he always walked on that Tanjong Rhu beach alone? Wasn't there a hand that he held onto? And crabs, she said – did she cook those crabs? Didn't she cook them in a big black pan?

And she said I used to count fishing boats even then. How old was I? When was all this? Why have I forgotten it all? I never asked her about it – not even then, when she talked about it, he thought sadly. I never sat down and talked to her. I never listened.

When he had tried, finally, to ask her, she was unable to answer. Deathly ill in hospital, she lay in bed, not moving, tied to machines which fed her, or gave her blood, or carried a tea-coloured urine away into a bag, drop by drop. The skin on her face looked like a fruit left to dry too long in the sun.

His daughter Ying was there, brushing the thin grey hair back from her grandmother's ears. She smiled at him.

'Popo's better today,' she said. 'She drank some chicken soup and I gave some blood for her.'

He put down the basket of flowers he had brought, walked back to close the door, then decided to leave it open. Hospital rooms felt like a prison to him.

'She had lots of visitors today, and she recognized some of them,' Ying said. 'Second Aunt came with some thick shiny material for Popo's burial clothes. She wanted to leave it on Popo's bed, but I wouldn't let her. We argued about it. It's in the cupboard now.' Ying stopped and looked up at him, with worried eyes. 'She's not going to die, is she?'

He walked up to the bed. The room was airless and smelled of bodies. 'Can't you open the window?' he asked.

Ying got up and pushed open the window. Turning, she said, 'You haven't said hello to her yet. Maybe she'll recognize you. You should try it, Baba.'

'She's asleep,' he said.

'No, she isn't,' Ying said. 'She keeps her eyes closed all the time, that's all. I think she's too tired to open them. But she can see, if I hold them open. Watch.'

She moved behind her grandmother, and carefully pulled the eyelids up. The old woman's eyes stared out at him, like colourless stones.

'Go on, Baba. Say something, hurry!'

'Ah-Ma,' he began, feeling stupid. 'I'm here. Can you hear me?'

Her eyes looked into the distance, unseeing. Then, from deep inside her, from the body which had brought him into the world, a single sound came out. 'Ah-Wah,' she said, her voice deep and warm.

'See? See? She recognized you,' Ying said excitedly. 'Now ask her something. Talk to her.'

Ask her something. He wished Ying wasn't there. 'Ah-Ma,' he said slowly, 'Ah-Ma, when I was little . . .'

'Louder,' Ying whispered.

'When we lived at Tanjong Rhu, Ah-Ma, did you take me for walks? Did you count fishing boats with me?'

Like bits of colourless stone, those eyes.

And was it you who made toy boats out of pieces of wood for me? Did you cook the crabs we caught together? Was it you who began this game of counting ships, Mother, was it?

It was no use. He could say nothing, and she could see nothing.

He looked up at Ying and said angrily, 'Let go of her eyelids. She's not a toy.'

'But she likes—'

'Let go!'

Ying let both eyelids gently down.

'Don't you have any respect? She's your grandmother, not some toy to play with!' He was on safe ground now. 'Playing with her eyes like that when she's dying—'

'She's *not* dying!' Ying cried.

'You young people have no respect for—'

'I gave blood, didn't I? You old people just give her burial clothes!'

'Ying, that's enough!'

Father and daughter stared at each other for a long moment. In the silence, a low sound from the bed surprised them both. Li turned to his mother, and noticed that, very weakly, her fingers were moving, searching for something on the bed. He reached over and held them still.

'Ah-Wah,' she said, 'the key . . .'

He looked at Ying questioningly.

'She's worrying about her keys again,' Ying said in English. 'Something to do with those old boxes where she keeps all her rubbish.' Ying bent down to her grandmother's ear and said loudly in Cantonese, 'Listen, Popo. I know where your keys are. I'll bring them here for you tomorrow, all right?'

The old head turned restlessly from side to side. 'No,' the old woman managed to say, 'the key to the altar, it's hidden . . . In a special place.'

'She's tired,' Ying said to her father. 'Tell her to stop worrying. She'll listen to you.'

'Ah-Ma,' Li said, bending towards her. 'It's all right. You rest now. Sleep.' Still he felt her fingers moving under his. 'Don't worry, Mother. The key is safe.'

Soon her fingers stopped moving. He took his hand gently away. Lying on the grey blanket, her thin fingers looked like a piece of seaweed, left on the beach by the sea.

*One by one Mr Li pulled the drawers open,
but he could find no joss sticks.*

The darkness was deepening outside his office window. It was hard to tell where the sea ended and the sky began – there was only a thin silver line between them. Night and day, sea and sky, life and death – only the thinnest of lines separated them.

The altar, he suddenly thought. Like the horizon outside, the altar is the line between life and death. I had forgotten – I must take care of the altar. It is what she would want. Mr Li put down the binoculars and turned away from his office window. It was too dark now anyway, to see the silent ships out at sea.

I have to go home, he thought. I have to do that one last thing for her.

The altar room was cool and dark. Without the smell of fresh flowers and joss sticks, the room seemed empty. He turned on the electric candles, which gave a pink light.

His father's face stared out of the photograph up on the altar. Carefully, Mr Li put a photograph of his mother next to it.

There, it was done. She was up there now, next to his father. He stepped back and looked at them both.

'Ah-Ma,' he began, then stopped. Quickly he looked at the doorway and checked that there was no one there. Then he bent his head and shoulders and bowed deeply, once, twice, three times. Some joss sticks, he thought, I should light some joss sticks. He went to the desk. One by one he pulled the drawers open, but he could find no joss sticks.

There was one drawer which would not open. The joss

sticks, he thought, must be in there, with all the things that were most important to her. He pulled again at that drawer, harder this time, but it stayed shut. And then he realized that she always kept it locked. And he did not know where she hid the key.

Through the window a light evening wind blew in. He stayed there for a moment longer, looking at his mother's photograph.

'Ah-Ma,' he whispered. 'Ah-Ma, I saw Tanjong Rhu today.' His voice broke. He stood there, arms hanging at his sides, a 63-year-old man in a grey business suit. What am I doing, he thought, talking in an empty room to an old photograph?

Quickly he turned and walked out of the altar room, leaving the faces of his two parents shining in the warm light of the electric candles.

In the Mountains

RUTH PRAWER JHABVALA

A story from India, retold by Clare West

Family life is not always comfortable. There are quarrels, arguments, different opinions, especially between mothers and daughters. Sometimes the only answer is to escape.

Pritam escaped years ago, to a rough stone house high on a mountainside in the Himalayas. Here she lives a simple life, alone and carefree – except for once a year when her family feel they must pay her a visit . . .

When you live alone for most of the time and meet almost nobody, then you begin to take less care of your appearance. That was what happened to Pritam. As the years went by, her appearance became rougher and shabbier. Although she was still in her thirties, she stopped taking care of herself.

Her mother was just the opposite. She had smooth hair and soft skin, loved sweets and beautiful clothes, and always smelled of perfume. Pritam smelled of – what was it? Her mother could not decide what it was. Perhaps the smell came from Pritam's clothes, which she probably did not change as often as she should. Tears came to the mother's eyes. They were partly for what her daughter had become, and partly for the happiness of being with her again. She had not seen Pritam for many months.

She always cried when she met Pritam, and when she said goodbye to her. Pritam was moved by these tears. Now, to hide her feelings, she spoke roughly, and even gave the old lady a push towards a chair. 'Go on, sit down,' she said. 'I suppose you're dying for your cup of tea.' The mother took it gratefully. She loved and needed tea, and the journey up into the mountains had made her very tired.

But she could not enjoy it. Pritam's tea was always too strong. They were in this rough room, which had very little furniture, in a rough stone house on the side of a mountain. And there was Pritam herself. The mother had to work hard at holding the tears back.

'I suppose you don't like the tea,' Pritam said crossly. She watched closely while the mother bravely drank it up to the last drop, and Pritam refilled the cup. She asked, 'How is everybody? Same as usual? Eating, making money?'

'No, no,' said the mother, protesting against Pritam's opinion of the family.

'Aren't they going up to Simla this year?'

'On Thursday,' the mother said, looking uncomfortable.

'And stopping here?'

'Yes. For lunch.'

The mother kept her eyes down. She said nothing more, although there was more to say. First Pritam had to accept the idea of her family visiting for a few hours on Thursday. It was nothing new, because some of them always stopped there on their way up to Simla. There was a good hotel nearby. 'We could have our lunch very comfortably there,' they used to sigh to each other. But they knew they couldn't just drive past her house; it wouldn't be right. So every year they came to lunch with her, but no one looked forward to the visit. Sometimes there was even a quarrel; then they got quickly into their cars and drove away.

Pritam said, 'I suppose you'll go with them.' She went on, 'Why should you stay? What is there for you here?'

'I want to stay.'

'No, you love to be in Simla,' said Pritam. 'It's so nice, meeting everyone walking on the Mall, and having tea in Davico's. Nothing like that here. You even hate my tea.'

'I want to stay with you.'

'But I don't want you!' Pritam was laughing. 'If you're here, how will I keep all my big love affairs going?'

'What, what?'

Pritam was delighted. 'Oh no. I'm telling you nothing, because then you'll want to stay.' She added, 'You'll frighten poor Doctor Sahib away.'

'Oh, Doctor Sahib,' said the old lady, pleased to find that Pritam was no longer being serious. But she continued with disapproval, 'Does he still come here?'

'Well, what do you think?' Pritam stopped laughing now and looked hurt. 'If he doesn't come, then who will? Except some wild animals, perhaps. I know you don't like him. You'd prefer me to know only wild animals. And the family, of course.'

'When did I say I don't like him?' the mother said.

'Ah!' Doctor Sahib cried happily when he saw her.
'Mother has come!'

'People don't have to say. And other people can feel things even when no one says anything. Here.' Pritam took her mother's cup and, in revenge, filled it for the third time.

Actually, it wasn't true that the mother didn't like Doctor Sahib – she just disapproved of him. The next morning he came to visit, and, as usual, he didn't look like the kind of person who should meet any of her family socially. He was a very small man, shabby and even dirty. He wore a kind of suit, but it was in terrible condition, and so were his shoes. One eye of his glasses, for some reason, was blacked out with a piece of card.

'Ah!' he cried happily when he saw her. 'Mother has come!' And his happiness meant that she could not look disapprovingly at him.

'Mother brings us news from the great world outside. What are we, Madam and I? Just two mountain bears.'

They were sitting in the garden. The mother had not come out to enjoy the view, which was wonderful, but to get warm in the morning sun. Although it was high summer, she always felt very cold inside the stone house.

'Has Madam told you about our winter?' Doctor Sahib said. 'Oh, these two bears have had a hard time! Ask her.'

'His roof fell in,' Pritam said.

'One night I was sleeping in my bed. Suddenly – crash, bang! I thought all the mountains were falling on to my poor house. I said, "Doctor Sahib, your hour has come."'

'I told him, I told him all summer, "The first snowfall and your roof will fall in." And when it happened, he didn't know what to do! What a stupid man!'

'Madam took me in, and all winter she let me have my corner by her own fireside.'

The mother looked at them in great surprise.

'Oh yes, all winter,' said Pritam, laughing at her. 'And all alone, just the two of us. Why did you have to tell her?' she asked Doctor Sahib. 'Just look at her face. Now she's thinking we're lovers.'

The mother's face reddened, and so did Doctor Sahib's. He was silent for some time, his head bent. Then he said to the mother, 'Look, can you see it?' He pointed down the mountainside to his house, some way below Pritam's. It was very small, not much more than a hut. 'Madam had the roof mended and now I'm back there, safe in my own home.'

Pritam said, 'One day the whole place will come down, not just the roof, and then what will you do?'

He had no answer to give. He was an educated man, but it was not clear if he had actually been a doctor. There was some mystery about his past, and his family were clearly ashamed of him. They had brought him to the mountains, away from everyone they knew. They had made him promise never to return to Delhi, and in return they paid him a little money to live on. He had nowhere else to live, and no friends to help him, except Pritam.

Later, when he had gone, Pritam said, 'Don't you think I've got a good-looking lover?'

'I know it's not true,' the mother said. 'But other people, what will they think – you alone with him in the house all winter? You know how people are.'

'What people?'

It was true. There weren't any. This made the mother feel sad. She looked at the mountains reaching into the distance, and saw emptiness and loneliness. But Pritam's eyes were half shut with happiness as she looked at the same view, and saw birds flying high up in the clear mountain sky.

'I was waiting for you all winter,' the mother said. 'I had your room ready. Why didn't you come? Why stay here when you can be at home and live like everybody else?'

Pritam laughed. 'Oh, but I'm not like everybody else!'

The mother was silent. She knew that Pritam was different. When she was a girl, they had worried about her and also been proud of her. She had been a big, good-looking girl with her own opinions. People said it was a fine thing that a girl like Pritam could have a free life in India, just as in other places.

Now the mother decided to break the news. She said, 'He is coming with them on Thursday.'

'Who's coming with them?'

'Sarla's husband.' She did not look at Pritam.

After a moment's silence, Pritam cried, 'Let him come! They can all come – everyone's welcome. What's so special about him? What's so special about any of them? They can come, they can eat, they can go away again, and goodbye. Why should I care about anyone? And also you! You also can go – right now, this minute, if you like – and I'll stand here and wave to you and laugh!'

Trying to stop her, the mother asked, 'What will you cook for them on Thursday?'

That did stop her. For a moment she looked wildly at her

mother. Then she said, 'My God, do you ever think of anything except food?'

'I eat too much,' the old lady agreed. 'Dr Puri says I must eat less.'

▲▲

Pritam didn't sleep well that night. She felt hot. So she got up and walked round the house in her nightdress. Then she opened the door and went out. The night air was cool, and it made her feel better at once. She loved being out in all this vast silence. Moonlight lay on top of the mountains, and even those that were green seemed covered in snow.

There was only one light in all that darkness. It came from Doctor Sahib's house. Had he fallen asleep with the light on? Or was he awake, too excited by his reading to go to sleep? Pritam decided to go down and find out. The path was very steep, but she knew it well. She looked in at his window. He was awake, sitting reading at his table. She knocked on the glass, then went around to open the door.

At the sound of her knock, he had jumped to his feet. He stared at her, shaking and afraid, when she entered.

'If you're so frightened,' she said crossly, 'why don't you lock your door? Any kind of person can come in and do what he wants.' He was so small and weak – it would be easy for someone to come in and murder him.

But there he was, alive. And now that he was no longer surprised, he was laughing and happy to see her. With great politeness, he invited her to sit on his only chair. She sat down and pulled her nightdress over her knees.

'Look at me, in my nightie,' she said, laughing. 'If Mother

Pritam sat down in the only chair. 'Look at me,
in my nightie,' she said, laughing.

knew! But of course she's fast asleep in her bed. Why are you awake? Reading one of your stupid books again! You'll go crazy one day!'

Doctor Sahib loved reading. He believed very strongly in past births, and that everybody lived many lives as different people, even animals. He mostly read books about the past, wondering if he had lived in those times as somebody else.

'I'm reading a very interesting story,' he said. 'There is a married lady – a queen, in fact – who falls hopelessly in love with someone who can't love her back.'

'Hopelessly?'

'Yes. So it's a very sad story. Would you like me to read some of it to you?'

'What's the use? These aren't things to read in books but to live through in real life. Have you ever been hopelessly in love?'

He turned his face away, and now only the piece of card was looking at her. But it seemed full of meaning.

She said, 'There are people in the world who feel much more strongly than other people. Of course they must suffer. If you want something more than just eating and drinking . . . You should see my family. They care about nothing except enjoying life.'

'Mine are the same in every way.'

'There's one of them, Sarla. She's not a bad person, but there's no difference between her and an animal. Perhaps I shouldn't talk like this, but it's true.'

'It is true. And in their past births these people really were animals.'

'Do you think so?'

'Yes. But the queens and the really great people, they become – well, they become like you. Please don't laugh! I have told you before what you were in your last birth.'

She went on laughing. 'You've told me so many things.'

'All true. Because you have passed through so many lives. And in each one you were a highly developed soul, but you also had a difficult life, with sadness and suffering.'

Pritam had stopped laughing.

'It is what happens to all highly developed souls,' he said. 'It is the price they have to pay.'

'I know.' She sighed deeply.

'I think a lot about this problem. Tonight, before you came, I sat here reading my book. I'm not ashamed to say that I couldn't go on reading, because my tears made it impossible to see the words. Then I looked up and asked, "Oh, Lord, why must these good souls suffer so much, while others who are less good can enjoy themselves freely?"'

'Yes, why?' Pritam asked.

'I shall tell you.' He was excited now, and he looked at her fully. 'As I was reading about these two people who fought so bravely with their feelings, I thought of myself. Yes, I too, feel and suffer here alone in my small hut. I cry out in pain, and my suffering is terrible but also – oh, Madam – it is wonderful!'

Pritam looked at a crack that ran right across the wall. One more heavy snowfall, she thought, and the whole hut will come down. And all this time he sits here and talks rubbish and I listen to him! She got up quickly.

He cried, 'I have talked too much! You are bored!'

'Look at the time,' she said. She opened the door. Trees and mountains were appearing out of the milk-white light of early morning. 'Oh my God,' she said, 'it's time to get up. And I'm going to have an awful day today, with all of them coming.'

'They are coming today?'

'Yes, and you won't want to visit. They aren't your kind of people at all. Not one bit.'

He laughed. 'All right.'

'They aren't even mine,' she said, beginning the upward climb back to her house.

▲▲

Pritam loved to cook and was very good at it. She enjoyed preparing lunch for the family. They arrived in three cars, and suddenly the house was full of fashionably dressed people with loud voices. Pritam came running out of the kitchen, with a red face and untidy hair, and welcomed everyone, even Sarla and her husband Bobby. The mother thought the meeting went surprisingly well. Pritam and Bobby hadn't met for eight years – in fact, not since Bobby had married Sarla.

Soon they were all eating a vast, excellently cooked meal. Pritam went round, putting more food on their plates, delighted to see them enjoying her food. She hadn't changed her clothes, and her face was hot and dirty from the kitchen. The mother watched, and began to feel angry. She thought to herself, why should she be like a servant to them? What have they ever done for her? Then she saw Pritam putting

Pritam went round, putting more food on their plates,
delighted to see them enjoying her food.

rice on Bobby's plate. When he turned round to say how good it was, Pritam looked proud and pleased. This made the mother even angrier. She went into the bedroom and lay down on the bed, feeling ill. She shut her eyes and tried not to hear the happy sounds coming from the next room.

After a while Pritam came in and offered to bring her some food. 'I don't want it,' the mother said. Then suddenly she opened her eyes and sat up. 'You should give food to him,' she said. 'You should invite him too. Or perhaps you think he is not good enough for your visitors?'

'Who?'

'You know very well. You were with him all last night.'

Pritam threw a look over her shoulder at the open door, then went closer to her mother. 'So you pretended to be asleep and all the time you were spying on me.'

'Not like that, Daughter—'

'And now you're having dirty thoughts about me.'

'Not like that!'

'Yes, like that!'

Both were shouting. The noise next door had stopped. The mother whispered, 'Shut the door,' and Pritam did so.

Then the mother said in a gentle, loving voice, 'I'm pleased he is here with you. He's a good friend to you. That is why I said you should invite him. When other friends come, we should not forget our old friends. And,' she added, 'I think he doesn't often eat well.'

Pritam laughed. 'You should see what he eats!' she said. 'Before he came here, do you want to hear what he did? He used to go to the kitchens of the restaurants and ask for food. He ate unwanted food from people's plates like a dog. And you want a person like that to be my friend.'

She turned away from her mother's surprised, suffering face. She ran out of the room and, past all her visitors, out of the house. She climbed up a path to a little flat piece of ground, and lay down in the grass. Here she was as high as the tops of the trees and the birds that sang from them. It was one of her favourite places. The view looked the same as usual, except for the three cars outside her house. Then someone came out of the house and, reaching inside a car door, brought out a bottle. It was Bobby.

Pritam watched him, and threw a small stone that fell at his feet. He looked up. He smiled. 'Hi, there!' he called.

She waved to him to climb up to her. He thought for a moment, looking at the bottle and towards the house. But then he lifted his head in a way that she recognized, and began to pick his way along the path. She put a hand over her mouth to cover a laugh, while she watched him climb slowly towards her, bent over and using his hands. When he arrived, he threw himself on the grass beside her to rest.

She hadn't seen him for eight years, and since then her whole life had changed. But it didn't seem to her that he had changed all that much. Perhaps he was a little heavier, but it made him look good, more manly than ever.

'You're in very poor condition,' she said.

'Isn't it terrible?'

He sat up and put the bottle to his mouth. She watched him drink. He passed the bottle to her, and she put her mouth where his lips had been and drank. The whisky jumped up in her like fire. They had often sat like this together, passing a bottle of whisky between them.

He looked at the view, the way she had often seen him look at beautiful girls. 'Nice,' he said. 'A nice place. I like it. I'd like to live here.'

'You!' She laughed.

He made a serious face. 'I love peace and quiet. You don't know me. I've changed a lot.' He turned towards her, and for the first time she felt him looking full into her face.

She put up a hand and said quickly, 'I've been cooking all day.' He looked away, and this politeness hurt her more than anything. She said heavily, 'I've changed.'

'Oh no!' he said quickly. 'You're just the same.' He looked at her with wide open eyes, to show his honesty. It was how he always looked when he was lying, she remembered.

She said, 'Everyone will wonder where you are.'

'Who cares? I want to stay with you. I was so excited yesterday thinking, "Tomorrow I'll see her again." I couldn't sleep all night. No, really – it's true.'

Of course she knew it wasn't. He slept like a bear; nothing could wake him. She smiled at the idea.

He saw this and moved closer. 'I think about you very often,' he said. 'I remember so many things – you have no idea. All the talks we had. It was great.'

Once they had had a very fine talk about free love. They had gone to a place they knew, by a lake. At first they were laughing. But when they got deeper into their conversation about free love (they both believed in it), they became more and more serious. In the end they had nothing more to say,

Bobby turned towards her, and for the first time
Pritam felt him looking full into her face.

and sat there silently. Although the air was quiet and the water didn't move, it felt like a storm to them. Of course it was their hearts beating. It was the most wonderful time they had ever had in their whole lives. After that, every time they were alone together, the same storm broke out.

Now Bobby sighed. 'It's funny,' he said. 'I have this fantastic social life. I meet lots of people, but there isn't one person I can talk with, the way I talk with you.'

'And with Sarla?'

'Sarla's all right, but she isn't really interested in serious things. She never thinks about them. But I do.'

'Give me another drink,' she said, needing it.

He passed her the bottle. 'You know what I like to do very often? Just lie on my bed and listen to nice music on my cassette. And then I have a lot of thoughts.'

'What about?'

'Oh, all sorts of things. You'd be surprised,' said Bobby.

She was filled with feelings that she remembered from the past. Perhaps they were partly because of the whisky. Was he feeling the same way as her? She put out her hand to touch his face, which was rough and manly, and then his neck, which was soft and smooth. When she touched him, he fell silent. She left her hand lying on his neck, loving to touch it. He stayed silent. When at last she took her hand away, she noticed that he looked at it. The skin was rough and not very clean. She hid her hands behind her back.

Now he was talking again, and talking fast. 'Honestly, Priti, you're really lucky, living here. What fantastic views! Who lives there?' He was pointing at Doctor Sahib's house.

Pritam answered eagerly, 'Oh, I'm very lucky – he's so interesting. I'm sorry you can't meet him.'

'What a pity,' Bobby said politely. Down below, people were putting things in the cars, ready to leave.

'Yes, you don't meet people like him every day. He does a lot of reading and thinking, and that's why he lives up here. Because it's so quiet.'

Now people were coming out of the house, looking around and calling Pritam's name.

'They're looking for you,' Bobby said, getting up.

'You see, if you're a serious thinker, you need real peace and quiet.' She stood up and looked down at the people calling for her. 'Every time I wake up at night, I can see his light on. He's always studying some book.'

'Fantastic,' Bobby said, looking at the people below.

'He knows all about past lives. He can tell you what you were in your past births. He's told me what I was.'

'Really? Does he know about me too?'

'Perhaps. If you're interesting enough.' She started off down the steep path. The conversation came to an end, because Bobby had to be careful where to put his feet.

At the house, the family were pleased to see her. The old lady was being difficult. She had decided not to go to Simla with them, but to stay with Pritam.

Pritam went into the bedroom, shutting the door behind her. The mother was lying on the bed, her face to the wall.

'If you stay, you'll have to have a cold bath every day.'

'I don't need hot water. If you don't need it, I don't.'

'And there's no Dr Puri here, if you get ill.'

'There *is* a doctor,' said the mother weakly.

'God help us!' Pritam said, and laughed out loud, but not unkindly. She opened the door to leave.

'Did you keep any food for him?' the mother said.

'There's enough to last him a week.'

She went out and told the others that her mother was staying. They did not argue for long – all they wanted was to get away as quickly as possible. As they drove away, they waved at her from the car windows. 'No quarrel this time,' they told each other. 'I think she's getting better, as she gets older, don't you?'

Pritam waited for the cars to reach the corner, and then she threw three stones. Each one hit the roof of a different car, one after the other. They'll wonder what's hit them, she thought, laughing to herself.

She picked up another stone and threw it all the way down at Doctor Sahib's roof. It landed with a loud noise, and he came running out. He looked straight up to where she was standing.

She put her hands to her mouth and called, 'Food!' He waved happily back, and immediately started up the well-known path. He climbed it as easily as she did.

GLOSSARY

altar a holy table in a holy place like a church, etc.
appearance what someone or something looks like
barracks a large building where soldiers live
bear (*n*) a heavy wild animal with thick fur and sharp claws
binoculars special glasses for seeing the details of distant objects
birth the time when a baby is born
blank empty-looking
bow (*v*) to bend your head down as a sign of respect
brick a hard block of clay used for building
candle a round stick of wax which burns to give light
Cantonese a language spoken mainly in south-east China
cataract a condition of the eye that can cause blindness
coffin a box in which a dead person is buried
commissar an officer of the Communist Party
complain to say you are unhappy or annoyed about something
crab a sea animal with a hard shell and eight legs, which moves
    sideways on land
crack (*n*) a line on the surface of something which has broken
director the head of an office or a department
disapprove to think that someone or something is not good or
    suitable; **disapproval** (*n*)
division (here) a unit of an army, a large number of soldiers
drawer a part of a desk, used for keeping things in
dye (*v*) to change the colour of something
eager very interested and enthusiastic about something that you
    want to do
educate to teach someone over a period of time
exercise (*n*) physical activity that you do to stay healthy

eyelid the piece of skin that moves to cover your eye

feed (*v*) to give food to people or animals

feeling something (e.g. anger, fear) that you feel inside yourself

frown (*v*) to make a serious, angry or worried expression by bringing your eyebrows closer together

harbour a place on the coast, where ships can stop safely

hut a very small, simple building

inherit to receive money or property from someone when they die

joss sticks thin wooden sticks covered with a substance that burns slowly and produces a sweet smell

liquid diet drinking liquids only and eating no solid food

local government the group of people who control the part of the country where you live

loose not tied tightly

love affair a sexual relationship with a man or woman

marry off to find a husband or wife for someone, often quickly

operation when a person's body is cut open in hospital

parcel something that is wrapped in paper

perfume a liquid with a nice smell that you put on your body

protest (*v*) to say or do things that show you disagree with something

puzzled not able to understand or explain something

quarrel (*n*) an angry argument or disagreement with someone

rank (*n*) a certain level in a political party or the army

respect (*n*) politeness towards someone who is older than you

rough plain, basic; not smooth; not polite

Sahib a word used in India in the past, when speaking to an important man

sake / for old time's sake because of someone's memories of the past

seaweed a plant that grows in the sea, and is often found on the beach

shabby in poor condition; wearing old, worn clothes

shipyard a place where ships are built or repaired

sigh (*v*) to let out a long deep breath to show you are sad, tired, etc.

social connected with society and meeting people

soul the part of a human that some people believe does not die

stew (here) a dish of fish and vegetables cooked slowly

suffer to feel pain or sadness

toy a thing for a child to play with

urine the waste liquid that you get rid of from your body

vast very, very big

yard an area next to a building, usually with a wall around

ACTIVITIES

Before Reading

Before you read the stories, read the introductions at the beginning. Then use these activities to help you think about the stories. How much can you guess or predict?

1 *Flame* (story introduction page 1). What do you think happened in Nimei's past? Try to guess the right answer.

She didn't marry the other man because . . .

   1 he was too young.   3 he was already married.
   2 he didn't love her.   4 her mother asked her not to.

2 *Tanjong Rhu* (story introduction page 18). Why do Mr Li and his mother see the world in different ways? Discuss these statements, and say if you agree or disagree.

   1 Old people always think that life was better in the past.
   2 In eighty years the world has changed a lot.
   3 Only young people can understand modern ideas.

3 *In the Mountains* (story introduction page 37). What do Pritam and her mother usually argue about, do you think? Choose one answer each time.

   1 Pritam's love life / Pritam's money / Pritam's work
   2 Pritam's children / where Pritam lives / who Pritam has married / how many parties Pritam has

ACTIVITIES

After Reading

1 **Here are the thoughts of six characters (two from each story). Who is thinking, and at what point in the story?**

1 'The family will think I'm crazy to stay on. Perhaps I am! But she's my daughter after all, even if she can be a bit difficult sometimes. And luckily I brought enough of Dr Puri's medicine with me to last for several months.'

2 'Mmm – what a taste! It's out of this world! That young man really knows how to cook fish. It's very kind of him to do this. My good-for-nothing family doesn't do a thing!'

3 'They all say they're so sad now that she's dead, but do they really care? I was with her in hospital, I gave blood for her – I was there when she died! I'll never forget that . . .'

4 'Yes, I see, Lord, I have to accept suffering and pain because – wait a minute, the cars are moving off, I think. One, two, three, yes, they're all leaving! My goodness, was that her voice? Oh, what happiness there is in the world!'

5 'Too many people round my bed today. Talking and crying and arguing. I don't need them. I want to sleep, that's all. But first I must . . . I'll wait . . . when Ah-Wah comes . . .'

6 'Well, well, out running, is she? I've been telling her for years she should take some exercise. Perhaps she's started listening to me for once! Or is there some other reason?'

2 **Perhaps Nimei and Hsu Peng, in *Flame*, wrote to each other after the end of the story. Here are six possible letters, three by Nimei and three by Hsu Peng. Who wrote each one? Write in the names. Then put the letters into pairs that match, and say which letter in each pair is the reply.**

Letter 1 by _____

How could you be so cruel to me? You must know I wanted to see you again so much. Are you happy now that you've had your revenge?

Letter 2 by _____

Thank you so much for the fish and cooking oil. Of course I understand how busy you are, but my husband was sorry not to meet you. Please do come another time.

Letter 3 by _____

I made a mistake too. Falling in love with you was a stupid thing to do! But I soon forgot you. You married your cook (was that his job?), and I married a girl from a rich family.

Letter 4 by _____

I was so sorry not to see you. It was a very busy time for me. Perhaps I'll be able to visit another year. I hope you enjoyed the fish. Please give my respects to your husband.

Letter 5 by _____

I wanted to say sorry for the past. I made a bad mistake, and I wanted to tell you that. Why did I listen to my mother, and not my heart? I've been unhappy ever since.

Letter 6 by _____

You decided not to marry me. I call *that* cruel. Do you have any idea how miserable I was at the time? I wanted to make you suffer too!

3 **Perhaps, after his mother's death, Mr Li, in *Tanjong Rhu*, talks to one of his sisters, who lives abroad. Complete Mr Li's side of the conversation, using as many words as you like.**

SISTER: Did you and Ah-Ma talk about things before she died?

MR LI: No, and I feel bad about that. I never _____.

SISTER: Well, you're a busy man. You don't have a lot of free time, do you?

MR LI: And I was so impatient with her. One day _____.

SISTER: To your office? Why?

MR LI: She wanted to _____.

SISTER: But that was thirty years ago, at least!

MR LI: Yes, I know. She couldn't see _____ and she kept talking about _____. And I didn't _____.

SISTER: She was very old. The past was more important to her than the present.

MR LI: Yes, I understand that now. When she was in hospital, I tried _____, but she _____.

SISTER: You mustn't worry about it. It's too late now.

MR LI: Too late, yes. I was too late for the altar room as well.

SISTER: What do you mean?

MR LI: In hospital Ah-Ma tried _____.

SISTER: And you didn't know where this special place was?

MR LI: No. When I put her photograph up on the altar, I wanted to _____, but they were in _____.

SISTER: And you couldn't find the key.

MR LI: No. I failed her. I couldn't do _____.

SISTER: You didn't fail her, Ah-Wah. You were a good son to her, and she knew that.

4 In *In the Mountains*, what do you think happened between
   Pritam and Bobby in the past? Read these three different
   conversations, and choose one suitable word to fill each gap.
   Which explanation do you prefer, and why do you like it best?

   1 'Let me tell you what really _____. Pritam and Bobby were
      going to _____. Everything was going well, and the _____
      was arranged. But Sarla was looking _____ a husband, and
      she decided to _____ Bobby from Pritam. Poor Pritam had
      _____ idea what was going on.'

   2 'Now don't believe what other people _____ you. This is
      actually the true _____. Pritam and Bobby were madly in
      _____, but when there was talk of _____, his parents said
      no. Sadly, they _____ of Pritam's lifestyle. She was rather
      _____ when she was younger, we all _____ that.'

   3 'Pritam told me herself – nobody else _____ the truth. She
      loved Bobby, of _____. Who wouldn't? But he's so very
      _____ from her. She realized they would _____ be really
      happy together. So she _____ seeing him. Not long after,
      she _____ to the mountains, in order to _____ alone.'

5 Write a short description of the mother in each story. Choose
   suitable expressions from the list below.

   · loves clothes and perfume   · is calm and kind
   · likes remembering the past   · is careful with money
   · thinks feelings are not important · often cries
   · worries about what people think   · complains a lot
   · likes doing things in the right way · tries hard to be nice

6 **What did you think about these stories? Choose words or phrases, and complete the sentences in your own words.**

1 The *saddest / funniest* story was _____ because . . .
2 The person I *liked best / felt sorry for / felt angry with* was _____ because . . .
3 _____ was right when *he / she* _____ because . . .
4 The story I *liked best / liked least* was _____ because . . .
5 I *liked / didn't like* the ending of _____ because . . .

7 **Here is a short poem (a kind of poem called a haiku) about one of the stories. Which of the three stories is it about?**

Who cares about love?
Enough to eat, that's what counts.
I know I was right!

Here is another haiku, about the same story.

The dream is broken.
She never saw him again,
The love of her life.

A haiku is a Japanese poem, which is always in three lines, and the three lines always have 5, 7, and 5 syllables each, like this:

| Who | cares | a | bout | love | = 5 syllables
| E | nough | to | eat | that's | what | counts | = 7 syllables
| I | know | I | was | right | = 5 syllables

Now write your own haiku, one for each of the other two stories. Think about what each story is really about. What are the important ideas for you? Remember to keep to three lines of 5, 7, 5 syllables each.

ABOUT THE AUTHORS

HA JIN

Ha Jin (his real name is Xuefei Jin) was born in 1956 in Liaoning, northern China. In 1969, during the Cultural Revolution, he joined the People's Liberation Army and served in it for six years. After his military service he taught himself English, and gained a Bachelor's degree in English studies and a Master's degree in Anglo-American literature. He left China in 1985 and took up a scholarship at Brandeis University in the United States. He was studying there when in 1989 Tiananmen Square happened in Beijing. The Chinese government's reaction made him and his wife decide to stay in the United States. He supported his family by working in restaurants and as a night watchman in a factory. After gaining his Ph.D., he became a professor of English, first at Emory University in Atlanta, Georgia, and then at Boston University, Massachusetts.

Ha Jin has written three books of poetry, *Between Silences*, *Facing Shadows*, and *Wreckage*, and four volumes of short stories, *Ocean of Words*, *Under the Red Flag*, *The Bridegroom* (2000), from which this story is taken, and *A Good Fall* (2009). He has also written five novels, *In the Pond*, *Waiting*, *The Crazed*, *War Trash*, *A Free Life*, and a book of essays, *The Writer as Migrant*. He has won many awards for his writing.

This is his view of writing: 'Good writers should observe and tell the story . . . The narrator shouldn't be intrusive. You have to respect the intelligence of the reader. The reader will always have their own interpretations.' He plans to keep writing. 'I think I've gone so far along this road that I can't just change. When I made the decision to write in English only, I was determined to travel all the way, no matter how tough, how solitary it was. I have to go to the end, see what I can do.'

MINFONG HO

Minfong Ho was born in 1951 to Chinese parents in Burma (now Myanmar), and now lives in upstate New York with her husband and three children. A Singapore citizen, she grew up in Thailand, and at sixteen left to study in Tunghai University in Taiwan. After that, she attended Cornell University in the USA, graduating with a BA and later an MFA. She says: 'I started to write only after I left home, as a way to conjure up Thailand for myself, to combat homesickness while studying abroad.'

Her first book, *Sing to the Dawn*, was published in 1975, and was later made into a musical and then a full-length animation film. Three other novels, *Rice Without Rain*, *The Clay Marble*, and *The Stone Goddess* draw upon her experiences teaching in northern Thailand and working with Khmer refugees on the Thai-Cambodian border. An anthology of her short stories, *Journeys*, was published in 2008.

Her picture books for young children include *Hush! A Thai Lullaby*, *Peek! A Thai Hide-and-Seek*, *Maples in the Mist: Translations of Tang Poems*, and *Brother Rabbit: A Cambodian Folktale*. She has won several awards for her writing, including the Caldecott Honor Award and the Southeast Asia WRITE award.

Minfong speaks three languages, and has said that Chinese is the language of her heart, Thai the language of her hands, and English the language of her head. Although she writes in English, she says that 'even now, when I cry, I cry in Chinese.'

Her experience of life is wide. She has worked in prisons and factories; she has planted rice seedlings, and spoken at international conferences in grand hotels. She says, 'There is so much, so much beauty and so much pain in the world around me which I want to write about – because I want to share it.'

RUTH PRAWER JHABVALA

Ruth Prawer Jhabvala was born in 1927 in Germany, of Polish parents. Her first stories were written in German, but when her family moved to England in 1939, she quickly made the change to a new language. After graduating from the University of London, she married an Indian architect and moved to Delhi, where she had three daughters, and wrote eight novels based on her experience of life in India. The first ten years of India, she has said, were wonderful, but then she became homesick for Europe and began to write more like an outsider, looking at the country and its people from a distance.

Her twelve novels and several collections of short stories have been highly praised. In 1963 she wrote her first screenplay, based on her own novel *The Householder*, for a film directed by James Ivory. Since then she has written screenplays for many successful films made by the Merchant–Ivory team: *Shakespeare Wallah*, *Quartet*, *A Room with a View*, *Howards End*, *The Remains of the Day*, *Surviving Picasso*, *The Golden Bowl* and *The City of Your Final Destination*. In 1975 she won the Booker Prize for her best-known novel, *Heat and Dust*, and spent the prize money on an apartment in New York. She and her husband now live in New York, making a yearly visit to India.

In the Mountains first appeared in *The New Yorker* magazine, and was later published in the short story collection, *Out of India*, which was chosen by *The New York Review of Books* as one of the Best Books of 1986.

During her lifetime Jhabvala has had to learn to live, as an outsider, in many different cultures, both eastern and western. She does not call any one country 'home' and says of herself: 'I'm absolutely passive, like blotting paper,' and, 'Not really having a world of my own, I made up for my disinheritance by absorbing the worlds of others.'

OXFORD BOOKWORMS LIBRARY

Classics • Crime & Mystery • Factfiles • Fantasy & Horror
Human Interest • Playscripts • Thriller & Adventure
True Stories • World Stories

The OXFORD BOOKWORMS LIBRARY provides enjoyable reading in English, with a wide range of classic and modern fiction, non-fiction, and plays. It includes original and adapted texts in seven carefully graded language stages, which take learners from beginner to advanced level. An overview is given on the next pages.

All Stage 1 titles are available as audio recordings, as well as over eighty other titles from Starter to Stage 6. All Starters and many titles at Stages 1 to 4 are specially recommended for younger learners. Every Bookworm is illustrated, and Starters and Factfiles have full-colour illustrations.

The OXFORD BOOKWORMS LIBRARY also offers extensive support. Each book contains an introduction to the story, notes about the author, a glossary, and activities. Additional resources include tests and worksheets, and answers for these and for the activities in the books. There is advice on running a class library, using audio recordings, and the many ways of using Oxford Bookworms in reading programmes. Resource materials are available on the website <www.oup.com/bookworms>.

The *Oxford Bookworms Collection* is a series for advanced learners. It consists of volumes of short stories by well-known authors, both classic and modern. Texts are not abridged or adapted in any way, but carefully selected to be accessible to the advanced student.

You can find details and a full list of titles in the *Oxford Bookworms Library Catalogue* and *Oxford English Language Teaching Catalogues*, and on the website <www.oup.com/bookworms>.

THE OXFORD BOOKWORMS LIBRARY
GRADING AND SAMPLE EXTRACTS

STARTER • 250 HEADWORDS

present simple – present continuous – imperative –
can/*cannot, must* – *going to* (future) – simple gerunds …

Her phone is ringing – but where is it?

Sally gets out of bed and looks in her bag. No phone.
She looks under the bed. No phone. Then she looks behind
the door. There is her phone. Sally picks up her phone and
answers it. *Sally's Phone*

STAGE 1 • 400 HEADWORDS

… past simple – coordination with *and*, *but*, *or* –
subordination with *before, after, when, because, so* …

I knew him in Persia. He was a famous builder and I
worked with him there. For a time I was his friend, but
not for long. When he came to Paris, I came after him –
I wanted to watch him. He was a very clever, very dangerous
man. *The Phantom of the Opera*

STAGE 2 • 700 HEADWORDS

… present perfect – *will* (future) – *(don't) have to, must not, could* –
comparison of adjectives – simple *if* clauses – past continuous –
tag questions – *ask*/*tell* + infinitive …

While I was writing these words in my diary, I decided
what to do. I must try to escape. I shall try to get down the
wall outside. The window is high above the ground, but
I have to try. I shall take some of the gold with me – if I
escape, perhaps it will be helpful later. *Dracula*

STAGE 3 • 1000 HEADWORDS

… should, may – present perfect continuous – *used to* – past perfect –
causative – relative clauses – indirect statements …

Of course, it was most important that no one should see
Colin, Mary, or Dickon entering the secret garden. So Colin
gave orders to the gardeners that they must all keep away
from that part of the garden in future. *The Secret Garden*

STAGE 4 • 1400 HEADWORDS

… past perfect continuous – passive (simple forms) –
would conditional clauses – indirect questions –
relatives with *where/when* – gerunds after prepositions/phrases …

I was glad. Now Hyde could not show his face to the world
again. If he did, every honest man in London would be
proud to report him to the police. *Dr Jekyll and Mr Hyde*

STAGE 5 • 1800 HEADWORDS

… future continuous – future perfect –
passive (modals, continuous forms) –
would have conditional clauses – modals + perfect infinitive …

If he had spoken Estella's name, I would have hit him. I was so
angry with him, and so depressed about my future, that I could
not eat the breakfast. Instead I went straight to the old house.
Great Expectations

STAGE 6 • 2500 HEADWORDS

… passive (infinitives, gerunds) – advanced modal meanings –
clauses of concession, condition

When I stepped up to the piano, I was confident. It was as if I
knew that the prodigy side of me really did exist. And when I
started to play, I was so caught up in how lovely I looked that
I didn't worry how I would sound. *The Joy Luck Club*

MORE WORLD STORIES FROM BOOKWORMS

The Meaning of Gifts: Stories from Turkey
STAGE 1   RETOLD BY JENNIFER BASSETT

———

Cries from the Heart: Stories from Around the World*
STAGE 2   RETOLD BY JENNIFER BASSETT

Changing their Skies: Stories from Africa
STAGE 2   RETOLD BY JENNIFER BASSETT

———

The Long White Cloud: Stories from New Zealand
STAGE 3   RETOLD BY CHRISTINE LINDOP

Dancing with Strangers: Stories from Africa*
STAGE 3   RETOLD BY CLARE WEST

Playing with Fire: Stories from the Pacific Rim*
STAGE 3   RETOLD BY JENNIFER BASSETT

A Cup of Kindness: Stories from Scotland
STAGE 3   RETOLD BY JENNIFER BASSETT

———

Doors to a Wider Place: Stories from Australia
STAGE 4   RETOLD BY CHRISTINE LINDOP

Land of my Childhood: Stories from South Asia**
STAGE 4   RETOLD BY CLARE WEST

The Price of Peace: Stories from Africa
STAGE 4   RETOLD BY CHRISTINE LINDOP

———

Treading on Dreams: Stories from Ireland
STAGE 5   RETOLD BY CLARE WEST

** Winner: Language Learner Literature Awards

* Finalist: Language Learner Literature Awards